Chapter 1: Introduction to AI and Python

Artificial intelligence (AI) has become an integral part of modern technology, transforming industries and revolutionizing the way we interact with the world. At its core, AI aims to create systems that can perform tasks that typically require human intelligence, such as understanding natural language, recognizing patterns, and making decisions. Python has emerged as a powerful and versatile programming language for AI development due to its simplicity, extensive libraries, and active community support.

In this chapter, we embark on a journey to explore the fundamentals of AI and understand why Python is the preferred choice for AI projects. AI encompasses a wide range of techniques, including machine learning (ML), deep learning (DL), reinforcement learning (RL), computer vision (CV), natural language processing (NLP), and large language models (LLM). Each of these techniques has its own unique applications and challenges, which we will delve into in the subsequent chapters.

Python's popularity in AI can be attributed to several factors. First, its syntax is easy to learn and read, making it accessible to both beginners and experienced programmers. Python's extensive library ecosystem provides a wealth of tools and frameworks specifically designed for AI development. Libraries such as NumPy, pandas, scikit-learn, TensorFlow, Keras, PyTorch, and OpenCV offer powerful functionalities for data manipulation, model building, and computer vision tasks.

To get started with Python for AI, it is essential to set up the right development environment. Anaconda, a popular distribution, simplifies the installation of Python and its associated libraries. Jupyter Notebooks provide an interactive platform for coding, visualization, and documentation, making them ideal for experimentation and learning. Additionally, version control systems like Git help manage code changes and collaborate with others effectively.

Once the environment is set up, we can begin by exploring the basics of Python programming. Understanding data types, control structures, functions, and object-oriented programming is crucial for developing AI applications. Python's versatility allows us to handle various data formats, perform mathematical operations, and manipulate data efficiently. With these foundational skills in place, we can move on to more advanced AI concepts and techniques.

In conclusion, this chapter has introduced the fundamental concepts of AI and highlighted the advantages of using Python for AI development. With its simplicity, extensive libraries, and active community support, Python has become the language of choice for AI practitioners. By setting up the right development environment and mastering the basics of Python programming, readers will be well-equipped to embark on their AI journey. In the subsequent chapters, we will delve deeper into specific AI techniques and explore their practical applications with detailed Python examples.

Chapter 2:
Machine Learning
Fundamentals

Machine learning (ML) is a subset of artificial intelligence that focuses on developing algorithms that enable computers to learn from and make predictions based on data. Unlike traditional programming, where explicit instructions are given to perform a task, machine learning algorithms identify patterns and relationships within data to make decisions or predictions. This chapter delves into the fundamental concepts of machine learning, providing a solid foundation for understanding and applying various ML techniques.

At the heart of machine learning lies the concept of data. Data serves as the fuel that powers ML algorithms, and its quality and quantity directly impact the performance of these algorithms. Data can be categorized into different types, such as structured data, which includes tabular data with rows and columns, and unstructured data, such as text, images, and audio. Understanding the nature of the data and the problem at hand is crucial for selecting the appropriate ML technique.

Supervised learning is one of the most common types of machine learning, where the algorithm is trained on labeled data. Labeled data consists of input-output pairs, where the output is known and used to guide the learning process. Regression and classification are two primary tasks in supervised learning. Regression involves predicting a continuous value, such as predicting house prices based on features like size and location. Classification, on the other hand, involves predicting discrete categories, such as determining whether an email is spam or not.

Unsupervised learning, in contrast, deals with unlabeled data, where the goal is to find hidden patterns or structures within the data. Clustering and dimensionality reduction are two key tasks in unsupervised learning. Clustering algorithms group similar data points together, enabling tasks such as customer segmentation and anomaly detection. Dimensionality reduction techniques, such as Principal Component Analysis (PCA), help reduce the number of features in the data while retaining important information.

Reinforcement learning (RL) is a different paradigm within machine learning, where an agent learns to interact with an environment to maximize cumulative rewards. Unlike supervised and unsupervised learning, reinforcement learning focuses on sequential decision-making. The agent takes actions based on its current state, receives feedback in the form of rewards or penalties, and updates its policy to improve future actions. RL has been successfully applied in various domains, including robotics, gaming, and autonomous systems.

To implement machine learning algorithms, Python provides a wealth of libraries and frameworks. Scikit-learn is a widely used library that offers a comprehensive collection of ML algorithms, along with tools for data preprocessing, model evaluation, and hyperparameter tuning. TensorFlow and PyTorch are powerful frameworks for building and training deep learning models, which are a subset of machine learning models inspired by the structure and function of the human brain.

In conclusion, machine learning is a powerful and versatile field within artificial intelligence that enables computers to learn from data and make predictions. By understanding the fundamental concepts of supervised, unsupervised, and reinforcement learning, readers will be well-equipped to tackle a wide range of ML problems. With the help of Python and its extensive libraries, implementing and experimenting with machine learning algorithms becomes accessible and efficient. In the subsequent chapters, we will delve deeper into specific machine learning techniques and explore their practical applications with detailed Python examples.

Training a neural network involves adjusting the weights and biases of the connections to minimize the error between the predicted and actual outputs. This process is achieved through backpropagation, where the error is propagated backward through the network, and the weights are updated using optimization algorithms such as gradient descent. The learning rate, which controls the step size of the weight updates, is a crucial hyperparameter that affects the convergence and performance of the model.

Deep learning models, also known as deep neural networks (DNNs), typically consist of multiple hidden layers, enabling them to learn hierarchical representations of the data. Convolutional neural networks (CNNs) are a specialized type of DNN designed for image processing tasks. CNNs utilize convolutional layers, which apply filters to the input data to extract spatial features, followed by pooling layers that reduce the dimensionality of the data. This architecture allows CNNs to capture local patterns and achieve state-of-the-art performance in image recognition tasks.

Recurrent neural networks (RNNs) are another type of DNN designed for sequential data, such as time series or text. RNNs incorporate feedback connections that allow information to persist across time steps, enabling the model to capture temporal dependencies. Long short-term memory (LSTM) networks and gated recurrent units (GRUs) are variants of RNNs that address the issue of vanishing gradients and improve the model's ability to learn long-term dependencies.

To implement deep learning models, Python provides powerful frameworks such as TensorFlow and PyTorch. TensorFlow, developed by Google, offers a flexible and scalable platform for building and training neural networks. Its high-level API, Keras, simplifies the process of creating and experimenting with deep learning models. PyTorch, developed by Facebook, is known for its dynamic computation graph and ease of use, making it a popular choice for research and development.

In conclusion, deep learning is a powerful and versatile field within artificial intelligence that enables the learning of complex patterns and representations from data. By understanding the fundamental concepts of neural networks, convolutional neural networks, and recurrent neural networks, readers will be well-equipped to tackle a wide range of deep learning problems. With the help of Python and its powerful frameworks, implementing and experimenting with deep learning models becomes accessible and efficient. In the subsequent chapters, we will delve deeper into specific deep learning techniques and explore their practical applications with detailed Python examples.

Chapter 4:
Convolutional
Neural Networks

Convolutional Neural Networks (CNNs) have revolutionized the field of computer vision, achieving state-of-the-art performance in tasks such as image classification, object detection, and image segmentation. CNNs are designed to process and analyze visual data by leveraging the spatial structure of images. This chapter delves into the fundamental concepts of CNNs, providing a comprehensive understanding of their architecture and applications.

At the core of CNNs lies the convolutional layer, which applies a set of learnable filters to the input image. Each filter slides over the image, performing a dot product between the filter and the local region of the image. This operation produces a feature map that captures local patterns and spatial relationships. The use of multiple filters allows CNNs to learn a diverse set of features, such as edges, textures, and shapes.

Pooling layers, also known as subsampling or downsampling layers, are used to reduce the spatial dimensions of the feature maps while retaining the most important information. Max pooling, the most common type of pooling, selects the maximum value within a local region, effectively reducing the size of the feature map. Pooling layers help to achieve spatial invariance, meaning the model becomes more robust to variations in the input image, such as translations and rotations.

The combination of convolutional and pooling layers forms the backbone of CNNs, allowing them to capture hierarchical representations of the input data. The early layers of a CNN learn low-level features, such as edges and textures, while the deeper layers learn high-level features, such as objects and shapes. This hierarchical structure enables CNNs to excel in complex visual recognition tasks.

To implement CNNs, Python provides powerful frameworks such as TensorFlow and PyTorch. TensorFlow, developed by Google, offers a flexible and scalable platform for building and training CNNs. Its high-level API, Keras, simplifies the process of creating and experimenting with CNN architectures. PyTorch, developed by Facebook, is known for its dynamic computation graph and ease of use, making it a popular choice for research and development.

For image classification, we will start with a simple CNN architecture and train it on the MNIST dataset, which consists of handwritten digits. We will explore techniques such as data augmentation and regularization to improve the model's performance and prevent overfitting. Next, we will implement a more complex CNN architecture for object detection using the YOLO (You Only Look Once) algorithm. This example will demonstrate how to detect and localize multiple objects within an image.

In conclusion, Convolutional Neural Networks are a powerful and versatile tool for computer vision tasks. By understanding the fundamental concepts of convolutional layers, pooling layers, and hierarchical feature learning, readers will be well-equipped to tackle a wide range of visual recognition problems. With the help of Python and its powerful frameworks, implementing and experimenting with CNNs becomes accessible and efficient. In the subsequent chapters, we will delve deeper into specific computer vision techniques and explore their practical applications with detailed Python examples.

Chapter 5: Recurrent Neural Networks

Recurrent Neural Networks (RNNs) are a class of neural networks designed to handle sequential data, making them ideal for tasks such as time series prediction, natural language processing, and speech recognition. RNNs incorporate feedback connections that allow information to persist across time steps, enabling the model to capture temporal dependencies. This chapter delves into the fundamental concepts of RNNs, providing a comprehensive understanding of their architecture and applications.

The key feature of RNNs is their ability to maintain a hidden state that captures information about previous time steps. At each time step, the hidden state is updated based on the current input and the previous hidden state. This recurrent structure allows RNNs to process sequences of varying lengths and capture dependencies across time. However, training RNNs can be challenging due to issues such as vanishing and exploding gradients.

Long Short-Term Memory (LSTM) networks and Gated Recurrent Units (GRUs) are variants of RNNs that address the issue of vanishing gradients and improve the model's ability to learn long-term dependencies. LSTMs introduce memory cells that can store information for long periods, controlled by input, output, and forget gates. These gates regulate the flow of information, allowing the model to selectively retain or discard information as needed. GRUs simplify the LSTM architecture by combining the forget and input gates into a single update gate.

RNNs can be applied to a wide range of tasks involving sequential data. In time series prediction, RNNs can be used to forecast future values based on historical data. For natural language processing (NLP), RNNs can be used for tasks such as text generation, sentiment analysis, and machine translation. In speech recognition, RNNs can process audio signals to transcribe spoken language into text.

To implement RNNs, Python provides powerful frameworks such as TensorFlow and PyTorch. TensorFlow, developed by Google, offers a flexible and scalable platform for building and training RNNs. Its high-level API, Keras, simplifies the process of creating and experimenting with RNN architectures. PyTorch, developed by Facebook, is known for its dynamic computation graph and ease of use, making it a popular choice for research and development.

For time series prediction, we will start with a simple RNN architecture and train it on a dataset of historical stock prices. We will explore techniques such as sliding window and sequence-to-sequence modeling to improve the model's performance. Next, we will implement an LSTM-based model for text generation using the Shakespeare dataset. This example will demonstrate how to generate coherent and contextually relevant text based on the input sequence.

In conclusion, Recurrent Neural Networks are a powerful and versatile tool for processing sequential data. By understanding the fundamental concepts of hidden states, LSTMs, and GRUs, readers will be well-equipped to tackle a wide range of tasks involving temporal dependencies. With the help of Python and its powerful frameworks, implementing and experimenting with RNNs becomes accessible and efficient. In the subsequent chapters, we will delve deeper into specific natural language processing techniques and explore their practical applications with detailed Python examples.

Chapter 6:
Natural Language
Processing with
Python

Natural Language Processing (NLP) is a subfield of artificial intelligence that focuses on the interaction between computers and human language. NLP techniques enable computers to understand, interpret, and generate human language, making them essential for tasks such as text analysis, machine translation, and sentiment analysis. This chapter delves into the fundamental concepts of NLP and provides practical examples of implementing NLP techniques using Python.

One of the key challenges in NLP is the representation of text data in a format that can be processed by machine learning algorithms. Tokenization is the process of breaking down text into individual words or tokens. Various techniques, such as word-level and subword-level tokenization, are used to handle different languages and text formats. Once tokenized, text data can be converted into numerical representations using techniques such as Bag of Words (BoW), Term Frequency-Inverse Document Frequency (TF-IDF), and word embeddings.

Word embeddings are a powerful technique for representing words as dense vectors in a continuous vector space. Unlike traditional representations such as BoW, word embeddings capture the semantic relationships between words. Popular word embedding models include Word2Vec, GloVe, and FastText. These pre-trained models can be used to initialize the word embeddings in NLP models, improving their performance on various tasks.

One of the foundational tasks in NLP is text classification, where the goal is to categorize text into predefined labels. Text classification can be used for tasks such as spam detection, sentiment analysis, and topic categorization. Machine learning algorithms such as Naive Bayes, Support Vector Machines (SVM), and deep learning models such as Convolutional Neural Networks (CNN) and Recurrent Neural Networks (RNN) can be used for text classification.

Named Entity Recognition (NER) is another important NLP task, where the goal is to identify and classify named entities such as persons, organizations, and locations in text. NER models typically use sequence labeling techniques, such as Conditional Random Fields (CRF) and Bidirectional LSTM-CRF, to capture the dependencies between words in a sequence. NER is widely used in information extraction and knowledge graph construction.

To implement NLP techniques, Python provides powerful libraries such as NLTK, SpaCy, and Hugging Face's Transformers. NLTK (Natural Language Toolkit) offers a comprehensive suite of tools for text processing, including tokenization, stemming, and tagging. SpaCy is a fast and efficient library for industrial-strength NLP, providing pre-trained models for various languages and tasks. Hugging Face's Transformers library provides state-of-the-art pre-trained models for tasks such as text classification, NER, and machine translation.

For text classification, we will start with a simple Naive Bayes classifier and train it on the IMDb movie reviews dataset for sentiment analysis. We will then implement a more complex RNN-based model for text classification using the Twitter sentiment analysis dataset. For named entity recognition, we will use the CoNLL-2003 dataset and implement a Bidirectional LSTM-CRF model to identify named entities in text.

In conclusion, Natural Language Processing is a powerful and versatile field within artificial intelligence that enables computers to understand and generate human language. By understanding the fundamental concepts of tokenization, word embeddings, text classification, and named entity recognition, readers will be well-equipped to tackle a wide range of NLP problems. With the help of Python and its powerful libraries, implementing and experimenting with NLP techniques becomes accessible and efficient. In the subsequent chapters, we will delve deeper into specific NLP applications and explore their practical implementations with detailed Python examples.

Chapter 7: Reinforcement Learning

Reinforcement Learning (RL) is a branch of machine learning where an agent learns to make decisions by interacting with an environment to maximize cumulative rewards. Unlike supervised learning, where the model learns from labeled data, RL involves learning through trial and error. This chapter delves into the fundamental concepts of reinforcement learning, providing a comprehensive understanding of its architecture and applications.

At the core of RL is the agent-environment interaction. The agent takes actions based on its current state and receives feedback in the form of rewards or penalties from the environment. The agent's goal is to learn a policy that maximizes the total rewards over time. This interaction is often modeled as a Markov Decision Process (MDP), which consists of states, actions, rewards, and transitions.

Value-based methods and policy-based methods are two primary approaches to solving RL problems. Value-based methods, such as Q-learning, focus on estimating the value of each state-action pair. The agent learns a Q-value function that represents the expected cumulative rewards for taking a particular action in a given state. The policy is then derived by selecting actions that maximize the Q-value. Deep Q-Networks (DQNs) extend Q-learning by using neural networks to approximate the Q-value function, enabling the agent to handle large and complex state spaces.

Policy-based methods, on the other hand, focus on directly learning the policy that maps states to actions. The agent learns a policy function that maximizes the expected cumulative rewards. Policy Gradient methods, such as REINFORCE and Actor-Critic, are commonly used for this approach. Actor-Critic methods combine value-based and policy-based methods by using an actor network to select actions and a critic network to evaluate the actions.

In addition to these methods, RL also involves techniques such as exploration-exploitation trade-off, where the agent balances between exploring new actions and exploiting known actions that yield high rewards. Techniques such as epsilon-greedy and softmax are used to implement exploration strategies. RL also involves the use of discount factors to balance immediate and future rewards, as well as techniques such as experience replay and target networks to stabilize training.

To implement reinforcement learning algorithms, Python provides powerful libraries such as OpenAI Gym, TensorFlow, and PyTorch. OpenAI Gym provides a collection of environments for testing and benchmarking RL algorithms. TensorFlow and PyTorch offer flexible and scalable platforms for building and training RL models.

For training an agent to play a game, we will start with a simple Q-learning algorithm and train it on the CartPole environment from OpenAI Gym. We will then implement a Deep Q-Network (DQN) to handle more complex state spaces, such as the Atari game environments. For resource allocation, we will use a Policy Gradient method to optimize the allocation of resources in a simulated environment.

For training an agent to play a game, we will start with a simple Q-learning algorithm and train it on the CartPole environment from OpenAI Gym. We will then implement a Deep Q-Network (DQN) to handle more complex state spaces, such as the Atari game environments. For resource allocation, we will use a Policy Gradient method to optimize the allocation of resources in a simulated environment.

Chapter 8: Computer Vision with Python

Computer Vision (CV) is a subfield of artificial intelligence that focuses on enabling computers to interpret and understand visual information from the world. CV techniques are used in various applications, such as image classification, object detection, image segmentation, and facial recognition. This chapter delves into the fundamental concepts of computer vision and provides practical examples of implementing CV techniques using Python.

Image processing is a crucial aspect of computer vision, involving techniques to enhance, transform, and analyze images. Basic image processing operations include resizing, cropping, rotating, and flipping images. These operations can be performed using libraries such as OpenCV and Pillow. Image enhancement techniques, such as histogram equalization and filtering, are used to improve the quality and contrast of images.

Feature extraction is another important aspect of computer vision, where the goal is to identify and extract meaningful features from images. Traditional feature extraction techniques include edge detection, corner detection, and blob detection. These techniques help in identifying significant structures and patterns within images. Modern feature extraction techniques leverage deep learning models, such as Convolutional Neural Networks (CNNs), to learn hierarchical features directly from raw pixel data.

Object detection is a key task in computer vision, where the goal is to identify and localize objects within an image. Traditional object detection methods, such as the Viola-Jones algorithm, rely on handcrafted features and classifiers. Modern object detection methods, such as YOLO (You Only Look Once) and Faster R-CNN (Region-based Convolutional Neural Network), leverage deep learning to achieve high accuracy and real-time performance. These methods use CNNs to extract features and predict bounding boxes and class labels for objects within the image.

Image segmentation is another essential task in computer vision, where the goal is to partition an image into meaningful regions or segments. Semantic segmentation assigns a class label to each pixel in the image, while instance segmentation identifies and separates individual objects within the image. Modern segmentation methods, such as U-Net and Mask R-CNN, use deep learning to achieve state-of-the-art performance in segmenting complex scenes.

Facial recognition is a specialized application of computer vision, where the goal is to identify and verify individuals based on their facial features. Traditional facial recognition methods use techniques such as Eigenfaces and Fisherfaces to extract facial features and perform recognition. Modern methods, such as FaceNet and DeepFace, leverage deep learning to learn facial embeddings that capture unique and discriminative features for each individual.

To implement computer vision techniques, Python provides powerful libraries and frameworks such as OpenCV, scikit-image, and TensorFlow. OpenCV (Open Source Computer Vision Library) is a widely used library that offers a comprehensive collection of tools for image and video processing. Scikit-image provides a set of algorithms for image processing and computer vision tasks. TensorFlow, with its high-level API Keras, simplifies the process of building and training deep learning models for computer vision applications.

For image classification, we will start with a simple CNN architecture and train it on the CIFAR-10 dataset, which consists of 10 classes of images. We will then implement an object detection model using the YOLO algorithm and train it on the COCO (Common Objects in Context) dataset. For image segmentation, we will use the U-Net architecture and train it on the Pascal VOC dataset. For facial recognition, we will implement a deep learning-based approach using FaceNet and train it on the LFW (Labeled Faces in the Wild) dataset.

In conclusion, Computer Vision is a powerful and versatile field within artificial intelligence that enables computers to interpret and understand visual information. By understanding the fundamental concepts of image processing, feature extraction, object detection, image segmentation, and facial recognition, readers will be well-equipped to tackle a wide range of computer vision problems. With the help of Python and its powerful libraries, implementing and experimenting with computer vision techniques becomes accessible and efficient. In the subsequent chapters, we will delve deeper into specific computer vision applications and explore their practical implementations with detailed Python examples.

Chapter 9:
Time Series
Analysis with
Python

Time series analysis is a branch of statistics and machine learning that focuses on analyzing and forecasting data points collected over time. Time series data is prevalent in various domains, such as finance, economics, weather forecasting, and healthcare. This chapter delves into the fundamental concepts of time series analysis and provides practical examples of implementing time series techniques using Python.

One of the key challenges in time series analysis is handling the temporal dependencies in the data. Unlike traditional machine learning problems, where data points are assumed to be independent, time series data exhibits correlations across time. Techniques such as autocorrelation and partial autocorrelation are used to analyze the temporal dependencies and identify patterns in the data.

Trend, seasonality, and noise are three important components of time series data. The trend represents the long-term direction of the data, seasonality captures the periodic patterns, and noise represents the random fluctuations. Decomposing a time series into these components helps in understanding the underlying patterns and improving the accuracy of forecasting models.

Exponential smoothing is a widely used technique for time series forecasting. Simple Exponential Smoothing (SES) is used for forecasting time series data with no trend or seasonality. Holt's Linear Trend Model extends SES by incorporating a trend component, while Holt-Winters Seasonal Model further extends it by adding a seasonality component. These models use weighted averages of past observations to generate forecasts, with more recent observations given higher weights.

Autoregressive Integrated Moving Average (ARIMA) is another popular technique for time series forecasting. ARIMA models combine autoregression (AR), differencing (I), and moving average (MA) components to capture the temporal dependencies in the data. Seasonal ARIMA (SARIMA) extends ARIMA by incorporating seasonal components, making it suitable for data with seasonal patterns.

Machine learning techniques, such as Support Vector Machines (SVM) and neural networks, can also be applied to time series forecasting. Recurrent Neural Networks (RNNs), particularly Long Short-Term Memory (LSTM) networks, are well-suited for handling sequential data and capturing long-term dependencies. Convolutional Neural Networks (CNNs) can also be used for time series analysis by applying convolutional filters to extract features from the data.

To implement time series analysis techniques, Python provides powerful libraries such as Pandas, Statsmodels, and Prophet. Pandas is a versatile library for data manipulation and analysis, offering tools for handling time series data. Statsmodels provides a comprehensive suite of statistical models and tests for time series analysis. Prophet, developed by Facebook, is a robust tool for forecasting time series data with strong seasonal patterns and missing values.

For time series decomposition, we will start with a simple example using the air passenger dataset and decompose it into trend, seasonality, and noise components. For forecasting, we will implement various models, including Exponential Smoothing, ARIMA, and Prophet, and evaluate their performance on the same dataset. For anomaly detection, we will use machine learning techniques such as Isolation Forest and Autoencoders to identify outliers in the data.

In conclusion, Time Series Analysis is a powerful and versatile field within statistics and machine learning that enables the analysis and forecasting of temporal data. By understanding the fundamental concepts of autocorrelation, trend, seasonality, and forecasting models, readers will be well-equipped to tackle a wide range of time series problems. With the help of Python and its powerful libraries, implementing and experimenting with time series analysis techniques becomes accessible and efficient. In the subsequent chapters, we will delve deeper into specific time series applications and explore their practical implementations with detailed Python examples.

Chapter 10: Anomaly Detection with Python

Anomaly detection, also known as outlier detection, is a branch of machine learning that focuses on identifying rare and abnormal patterns in data. Anomalies can indicate critical events, such as fraud, equipment failures, or cybersecurity threats. This chapter delves into the fundamental concepts of anomaly detection and provides practical examples of implementing anomaly detection techniques using Python.

Anomalies can be broadly categorized into three types: point anomalies, contextual anomalies, and collective anomalies. Point anomalies refer to individual data points that deviate significantly from the rest of the data. Contextual anomalies, also known as conditional anomalies, occur when data points are considered anomalous in a specific context, such as time or space. Collective anomalies refer to groups of data points that deviate from the expected pattern.

Statistical methods are commonly used for anomaly detection, where the goal is to identify data points that deviate significantly from the statistical properties of the data. Techniques such as z-score, Grubbs' test, and the Mann-Whitney U test are used to identify point anomalies based on statistical measures. These methods assume that the data follows a specific distribution, such as normal distribution, and detect anomalies based on deviations from this distribution.

Machine learning techniques, such as clustering and classification, can also be applied to anomaly detection. Clustering algorithms, such as K-means and DBSCAN, group similar data points together, and data points that do not belong to any cluster are considered anomalies. Classification algorithms, such as Support Vector Machines (SVM) and Random Forests, can be trained on labeled data to distinguish between normal and anomalous patterns. Unsupervised techniques, such as Isolation Forest and Autoencoders, are used when labeled data is not available.

Isolation Forest is a popular unsupervised anomaly detection technique that isolates anomalies by recursively partitioning the data. The idea is that anomalies are more susceptible to isolation and require fewer partitions to be separated from the rest of the data. Autoencoders, a type of neural network, are trained to reconstruct the input data. Anomalies are detected based on the reconstruction error, as they are harder to reconstruct accurately.

To implement anomaly detection techniques, Python provides powerful libraries such as Scikit-learn, PyOD, and TensorFlow. Scikit-learn offers a wide range of machine learning algorithms for clustering and classification, as well as tools for evaluating anomaly detection models. PyOD (Python Outlier Detection) is a comprehensive library dedicated to anomaly detection, providing a variety of models and evaluation metrics. TensorFlow, with its high-level API Keras, simplifies the process of building and training neural network-based anomaly detection models.

For detecting fraudulent transactions, we will start with a simple example using statistical methods and the credit card fraud detection dataset. We will then implement machine learning-based approaches, such as Isolation Forest and Autoencoders, and evaluate their performance on the same dataset. For identifying equipment failures, we will use time series data from a predictive maintenance dataset and apply techniques such as clustering and classification to detect anomalies.

In conclusion, Anomaly Detection is a powerful and versatile field within machine learning that enables the identification of rare and abnormal patterns in data. By understanding the fundamental concepts of point anomalies, contextual anomalies, and collective anomalies, readers will be well-equipped to tackle a wide range of anomaly detection problems. With the help of Python and its powerful libraries, implementing and experimenting with anomaly detection techniques becomes accessible and efficient. In the subsequent chapters, we will delve deeper into specific anomaly detection applications and explore their practical implementations with detailed Python examples.

Chapter 11: Deep Reinforcement Learning

Deep Reinforcement Learning (DRL) combines the principles of reinforcement learning and deep learning to create powerful algorithms capable of solving complex decision-making problems. DRL has achieved remarkable success in various domains, such as playing video games, robotics, and autonomous driving. This chapter delves into the fundamental concepts of deep reinforcement learning and provides practical examples of implementing DRL algorithms using Python.

At the core of DRL is the combination of deep neural networks and reinforcement learning algorithms. Deep neural networks are used to approximate value functions, policies, or models of the environment. The use of neural networks allows DRL algorithms to handle large and complex state and action spaces, making them suitable for a wide range of applications.

One of the foundational DRL algorithms is Deep Q-Network (DQN), which extends the Q-learning algorithm by using a neural network to approximate the Q-value function. DQN introduces techniques such as experience replay and target networks to stabilize training and improve performance. Experience replay stores past experiences in a replay buffer and samples mini-batches for training, reducing the correlations between consecutive updates. Target networks, which are periodically updated with the weights of the Q-network, provide more stable targets for the Q-value updates.

Policy gradient methods, such as REINFORCE and Actor-Critic, are another class of DRL algorithms. These methods directly optimize the policy by estimating the gradient of the expected cumulative rewards with respect to the policy parameters. Actor-Critic methods combine the advantages of value-based and policy-based methods by using an actor network to select actions and a critic network to evaluate the actions. The actor network updates the policy based on the feedback from the critic network.

Advanced DRL algorithms, such as Proximal Policy Optimization (PPO) and Trust Region Policy Optimization (TRPO), introduce additional techniques to improve the stability and efficiency of training. PPO uses a clipped surrogate objective to constrain the policy updates, ensuring that they do not deviate too much from the current policy. TRPO uses a trust region constraint to ensure that the policy updates lead to a monotonically improving policy.

To implement DRL algorithms, Python provides powerful libraries such as TensorFlow, PyTorch, and OpenAI Baselines. TensorFlow and PyTorch offer flexible and scalable platforms for building and training neural networks, while OpenAI Baselines provides implementations of various DRL algorithms, making it easier to experiment with and benchmark different approaches.

For training an agent to play video games, we will start with a simple DQN algorithm and train it on the Atari game environments using the OpenAI Gym library. We will then implement more advanced algorithms, such as PPO and TRPO, and evaluate their performance on the same environments. For controlling robotic systems, we will use a simulated robot environment and apply DRL techniques to train the robot to perform tasks such as navigation and manipulation.

In conclusion, Deep Reinforcement Learning is a powerful and versatile field within artificial intelligence that combines the principles of reinforcement learning and deep learning to solve complex decision-making problems. By understanding the fundamental concepts of DQN, policy gradient methods, and advanced DRL algorithms, readers will be well-equipped to tackle a wide range of DRL problems. With the help of Python and its powerful libraries, implementing and experimenting with DRL algorithms becomes accessible and efficient. In the subsequent chapters, we will delve deeper into specific DRL applications and explore their practical implementations with detailed Python examples.

Chapter 12:
Natural Language
Processing
Applications

Natural Language Processing (NLP) has a wide range of applications, from text classification and sentiment analysis to machine translation and chatbots. This chapter explores various NLP applications and provides practical examples of implementing these applications using Python.

One of the most common NLP applications is text classification, where the goal is to categorize text into predefined labels. Text classification can be used for tasks such as spam detection, sentiment analysis, and topic categorization. Machine learning algorithms such as Naive Bayes, Support Vector Machines (SVM), and deep learning models such as Convolutional Neural Networks (CNN) and Recurrent Neural Networks (RNN) can be used for text classification.

Sentiment analysis is a specific type of text classification that focuses on identifying the sentiment or emotion expressed in a piece of text. Sentiment analysis can be used to analyze customer reviews, social media posts, and survey responses. Pre-trained models such as BERT (Bidirectional Encoder Representations from Transformers) can be fine-tuned for sentiment analysis tasks, providing state-of-the-art performance.

Machine translation is another important NLP application, where the goal is to automatically translate text from one language to another. Traditional machine translation methods, such as phrase-based translation, rely on statistical models to translate text. Modern methods, such as neural machine translation (NMT), use deep learning models such as sequence-to-sequence (Seq2Seq) with attention mechanisms to achieve high-quality translations. Pre-trained models such as Google's Transformer and Facebook's M2M-100 can be fine-tuned for specific translation tasks.

Named Entity Recognition (NER) is an NLP application that focuses on identifying and classifying named entities such as persons, organizations, and locations in text. NER models typically use sequence labeling techniques, such as Conditional Random Fields (CRF) and Bidirectional LSTM-CRF, to capture the dependencies between words in a sequence. NER is widely used in information extraction and knowledge graph construction.

Chatbots and virtual assistants are another popular NLP application, where the goal is to enable computers to interact with users in natural language. Chatbots can be used for customer support, personal assistants, and conversational agents. Techniques such as intent classification and entity recognition are used to understand user queries, while dialogue management and response generation are used to generate appropriate responses. Pre-trained models such as GPT-3 and T5 can be fine-tuned for chatbot applications, providing conversational capabilities.

To implement NLP applications, Python provides powerful libraries such as NLTK, SpaCy, and Hugging Face's Transformers. NLTK (Natural Language Toolkit) offers a comprehensive suite of tools for text processing, including tokenization, stemming, and tagging. SpaCy is a fast and efficient library for industrial-strength NLP, providing pre-trained models for various languages and tasks. Hugging Face's Transformers library provides state-of-the-art pre-trained models for tasks such as text classification, sentiment analysis, and machine translation.

For text classification, we will start with a simple Naive Bayes classifier and train it on the IMDb movie reviews dataset for sentiment analysis. We will then implement a more complex RNN-based model for text classification using the Twitter sentiment analysis dataset. For machine translation, we will use a Seq2Seq model with attention and train it on the WMT (Workshop on Machine Translation) dataset. For named entity recognition, we will use the CoNLL-2003 dataset and implement a Bidirectional LSTM-CRF model to identify named entities in text. For chatbot development, we will use the OpenAI GPT-3 model and fine-tune it for a customer support chatbot.

In conclusion, Natural Language Processing has a wide range of applications that enable computers to understand and generate human language. By understanding the fundamental concepts of text classification, sentiment analysis, machine translation, named entity recognition, and chatbot development, readers will be well-equipped to tackle a wide range of NLP problems. With the help of Python and its powerful libraries, implementing and experimenting with NLP applications becomes accessible and efficient. In the subsequent chapters, we will delve deeper into specific NLP applications and explore their practical implementations with detailed Python examples.

Chapter 13: Computer Vision Applications

Computer Vision (CV) has a wide range of applications, from image classification and object detection to image segmentation and facial recognition. This chapter explores various CV applications and provides practical examples of implementing these applications using Python.

Image classification is one of the most fundamental CV tasks, where the goal is to categorize images into predefined labels. Image classification can be used for tasks such as identifying objects in images, recognizing handwritten digits, and diagnosing medical conditions. Deep learning models such as Convolutional Neural Networks (CNN) are widely used for image classification, achieving state-of-the-art performance.

Object detection is a key CV application, where the goal is to identify and localize objects within an image. Object detection can be used for tasks such as detecting pedestrians in autonomous driving, identifying products in retail, and monitoring wildlife. Modern object detection methods, such as YOLO (You Only Look Once) and Faster R-CNN (Region-based Convolutional Neural Network), leverage deep learning to achieve high accuracy and real-time performance.

Image segmentation is another essential CV application, where the goal is to partition an image into meaningful regions or segments. Image segmentation can be used for tasks such as medical image analysis, autonomous driving, and scene understanding. Semantic segmentation assigns a class label to each pixel in the image, while instance segmentation identifies and separates individual objects within the image. Modern segmentation methods, such as U-Net and Mask R-CNN, use deep learning to achieve state-of-the-art performance in segmenting complex scenes.

Facial recognition is a specialized CV application, where the goal is to identify and verify individuals based on their facial features. Facial recognition can be used for tasks such as security and surveillance, access control, and social media tagging. Modern methods, such as FaceNet and DeepFace, leverage deep learning to learn facial embeddings that capture unique and discriminative features for each individual.

Generative Adversarial Networks (GANs) are another exciting application of computer vision, where the goal is to generate realistic images from random noise or other input data. GANs can be used for tasks such as image synthesis, style transfer, and data augmentation. Variants of GANs, such as CycleGAN and StyleGAN, have achieved remarkable success in generating high-quality and visually appealing images.

To implement CV applications, Python provides powerful libraries and frameworks such as OpenCV, scikit-image, and TensorFlow. OpenCV (Open Source Computer Vision Library) is a widely used library that offers a comprehensive collection of tools for image and video processing. Scikit-image provides a set of algorithms for image processing and computer vision tasks. TensorFlow, with its high-level API Keras, simplifies the process of building and training deep learning models for computer vision applications.

For image classification, we will start with a simple CNN architecture and train it on the CIFAR-10 dataset, which consists of 10 classes of images. For object detection, we will implement the YOLO algorithm and train it on the COCO (Common Objects in Context) dataset. For image segmentation, we will use the U-Net architecture and train it on the Pascal VOC dataset. For facial recognition, we will implement a deep learning-based approach using FaceNet and train it on the LFW (Labeled Faces in the Wild) dataset. For GANs, we will implement a simple GAN architecture and train it to generate handwritten digits using the MNIST dataset.

In conclusion, Computer Vision has a wide range of applications that enable computers to interpret and understand visual information. By understanding the fundamental concepts of image classification, object detection, image segmentation, facial recognition, and GANs, readers will be well-equipped to tackle a wide range of CV problems. With the help of Python and its powerful libraries, implementing and experimenting with CV applications becomes accessible and efficient. In the subsequent chapters, we will delve deeper into specific CV applications and explore their practical implementations with detailed Python examples.

Chapter 14: Reinforcement Learning Applications

Reinforcement Learning (RL) has a wide range of applications, from game playing and robotics to resource management and finance. This chapter explores various RL applications and provides practical examples of implementing these applications using Python.

One of the most well-known RL applications is game playing, where the goal is to train an agent to play and master various games. RL has achieved remarkable success in playing classic board games, such as chess and Go, as well as video games, such as Atari games and Dota 2. Algorithms such as Q-learning, Deep Q-Network (DQN), and AlphaGo combine RL and deep learning to achieve superhuman performance in game playing.

Robotics is another key RL application, where the goal is to train robots to perform tasks such as navigation, manipulation, and grasping. RL techniques such as Proximal Policy Optimization (PPO) and Soft Actor-Critic (SAC) can be used to train robots to learn complex behaviors through trial and error. Simulated environments, such as OpenAI Gym and MuJoCo, provide a safe and efficient way to train RL agents before deploying them in the real world.

Resource management is an RL application that focuses on optimizing the allocation and utilization of resources in various domains, such as cloud computing, telecommunications, and supply chain management. RL algorithms can be used to dynamically allocate resources based on changing demands, reducing costs and improving efficiency. Techniques such as Multi-Armed Bandits and Reinforcement Learning with Neural Networks (RLNN) can be applied to resource management problems.

Finance is another domain where RL can be applied to optimize trading strategies, portfolio management, and risk assessment. RL algorithms can be used to learn optimal trading strategies based on historical market data, maximizing returns and minimizing risks. Techniques such as Reinforcement Learning with Function Approximation and Deep Reinforcement Learning can be used to model complex financial markets and make informed decisions.

To implement RL applications, Python provides powerful libraries and frameworks such as OpenAI Gym, Stable Baselines, and RLlib. OpenAI Gym offers a diverse collection of environments for testing and benchmarking RL algorithms. Stable Baselines provides implementations of various RL algorithms, making it easier to experiment with and benchmark different approaches. RLlib, part of the Ray distributed computing framework, offers scalable and efficient tools for training RL agents in distributed environments.

For game playing, we will start with a simple Q-learning algorithm and train an agent to play the CartPole game using the OpenAI Gym environment. We will then implement more advanced algorithms, such as DQN and PPO, and evaluate their performance on the same environment. For robotics, we will use a simulated robot environment and apply RL techniques to train the robot to perform tasks such as navigation and manipulation. For resource management, we will implement a Multi-Armed Bandit algorithm to optimize the allocation of resources in a cloud computing environment. For finance, we will develop a trading strategy using a Deep Q-Network and evaluate its performance on historical market data.

In conclusion, Reinforcement Learning has a wide range of applications that enable agents to learn and make decisions in complex environments. By understanding the fundamental concepts of Q-learning, policy gradient methods, and advanced RL algorithms, readers will be well-equipped to tackle a wide range of RL problems. With the help of Python and its powerful libraries, implementing and experimenting with RL applications becomes accessible and efficient. In the subsequent chapters, we will delve deeper into specific RL applications and explore their practical implementations with detailed Python examples.

Chapter 41:
Large Language
Models (LLMs)

Large Language Models (LLMs) have revolutionized the field of Natural Language Processing (NLP) by demonstrating remarkable capabilities in understanding and generating human language. These models, powered by advanced deep learning techniques, have set new benchmarks in various NLP tasks, from translation and summarization to question-answering and conversational agents. This chapter delves into the intricacies of LLMs, their architecture, training methodologies, and practical applications, along with Python examples to illustrate their use.

Understanding Large Language Models

Large Language Models are built using transformer architectures, which have replaced traditional RNNs and LSTMs due to their superior performance in capturing long-range dependencies in text. The transformer model, introduced in the seminal paper "Attention is All You Need," employs a self-attention mechanism that allows it to weigh the importance of different words in a sentence, regardless of their distance from each other. This capability is crucial for understanding context and generating coherent text.

One of the most notable LLMs is GPT-3 (Generative Pre-trained Transformer 3), developed by OpenAI. With 175 billion parameters, GPT-3 has demonstrated unprecedented abilities in text generation, making it one of the largest and most powerful language models to date. Other significant models include BERT (Bidirectional Encoder Representations from Transformers), T5 (Text-to-Text Transfer Transformer), and the recently developed GPT-4.

Training Large Language Models

Training LLMs involves two main phases: pre-training and fine-tuning.

- Pre-training: In this phase, the model is trained on a massive corpus of text data using unsupervised learning techniques. The objective is to learn language representations that capture the nuances of grammar, semantics, and world knowledge. For instance, GPT-3 was pre-trained on a diverse dataset containing text from books, websites, and other text sources, allowing it to generate human-like text.

- Fine-tuning: After pre-training, the model undergoes supervised fine-tuning on specific tasks using labeled data. This phase adjusts the model's weights to optimize its performance on particular applications such as sentiment analysis, named entity recognition, or machine translation. Fine-tuning enables the model to apply its general language understanding to specialized tasks effectively.

Applications of Large Language Models

LLMs have a wide range of applications across various domains:

- Text Generation: LLMs can generate coherent and contextually relevant text, making them useful for content creation, storytelling, and automated writing assistants.
- Machine Translation: Models like GPT-3 and T5 have shown proficiency in translating text between languages with high accuracy.
- Conversational Agents: LLMs power advanced chatbots and virtual assistants, providing more natural and engaging interactions.
- Question-Answering: These models excel in extracting relevant information from large datasets, enabling them to answer questions accurately.
- Summarization: LLMs can condense lengthy documents into concise summaries, aiding in information retrieval and comprehension.

Python Example: Using GPT-3

To illustrate the use of LLMs, let's explore a simple Python example using GPT-3. We'll use the OpenAI API to generate text based on a given prompt.

```python
import openai
# Set your OpenAI API key
openai.api_key = 'your-api-key'
# Define a prompt for text generation
prompt = "Explain the significance of Large Language Models in NLP."
# Generate text using GPT-3
response = openai.Completion.create(
    engine="text-davinci-003",
    prompt=prompt,
    max_tokens=150
)
# Print the generated text
print(response.choices[0].text.strip())
```

In this example, we first set the API key for authentication with the OpenAI service. We then define a prompt that instructs GPT-3 to generate text explaining the significance of LLMs in NLP. The openai.Completion.create function generates a response based on the prompt, and we print the resulting text.

Future of Large Language Models

The development of LLMs is an ongoing process, with researchers continually pushing the boundaries of what these models can achieve. Future advancements may include models with even larger parameter counts, improved training techniques, and enhanced capabilities in understanding and generating human language. As LLMs become more accessible and integrated into various applications, their impact on industries such as healthcare, education, and entertainment will continue to grow, transforming the way we interact with technology.

In conclusion, Large Language Models represent a significant leap forward in the field of NLP. Their ability to understand and generate human language with high accuracy and coherence has opened up new possibilities for automation, content creation, and intelligent systems. By leveraging the power of LLMs, we can build more sophisticated and capable applications that enhance our interaction with technology and the digital world.